Welcome

Customer Service Excellence
Delighting Your Customers and Your Manager

Customer Service Excellence combines self-study with realistic workplace activities to build advanced knowledge of customer service principles. In a selling situation this Learning Short-take® helps to uncover customer needs and sell the value of the product on benefits rather than just price. In a customer service environment this Learning Short-take® helps to listen to the voice of the customer, responding to their stated needs and uncovering their unstated needs. Customer focused retail stores place customer needs at the heart of the selling process and aim to build customer loyalty, which increases the satisfaction levels for customers, employees and business owners. Furthermore, the components of what it takes to delight the customer are explored.

The people we need to build our business are out there. They are waiting to experience the good feelings that go with having their expectations met. They are constantly searching for satisfaction and recognition of their worth as customers. The great opportunity awaiting every business today is the chance to give excellent customer service that results in the customer coming back again and again.

The reliance on one method of customer service for different types of customers in different situations is limiting. Often,

1	**Participant Guide** > Start here
2	**Learning Journal** 55
3	**Skill Development Action Plan** 61
4	**Quick Reference** 67
5	**Next Step** 87

each customer's needs are different making every customer service interaction unique. **Customer Service Excellence** helps to identify common threads amongst customer interactions which can be applied to all situations, and also unique situations that often need to be addressed in the moment, without preparation. Understanding and using the core principles of this Learning Short-take® will help to navigate the known and the unknown when working with every customer.

Customer Service Excellence includes job aids for remembering the **Customer Satisfaction Model, 5-step Customer Service Model** and the **7-step Handling Difficult Situations Model** provided as free downloadable tools.

Now let's get started!

"Customer satisfaction is first and
foremost a state of mind and action…
an every minute of every day obsession."

Charles M, Cawley, President of MBNA America, Inc.

tpc™

The Performance Company

Delivering training solutions

Learning Short-take™

CUSTOMER SERVICE EXCELLENCE

Delighting your customers and your manager

CATHERINE MATTISKE

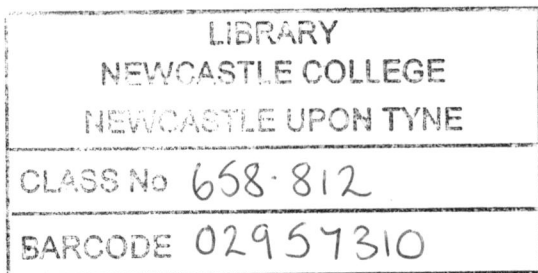

tpc™ The Performance Company
Delivering training solutions.

TPC - The Performance Company Pty Ltd
PO Box 639
Rozelle NSW 2039
Sydney, Australia

ACN 077 455 273
email: info@tpc.net.au
Website: www.tpc.net.au

National Library of Australia
Cataloguing-in-Publication data

Mattiske, Catherine
Customer Service Excellence: Delighting Your Customers and Your Manager

ISBN 978-1-921547-27-0

1. Occupational training 2. Learning I. Title

370.113

Printed in USA

Distributed by TPC - The Performance Company - www.tpc.net.au
For further information contact TPC - The Performance Company, Sydney Australia on +61 9555 1953 or TPC - The Performance Company, California on +1 (818) 824 6006, or email info@tpc.net.au

HELLO.

Welcome to the Learning Short-take® process!

This Learning Short-take® is a bite sized learning package that aims to improve your skills and provide you with an opportunity for personal and professional development to achieve success in your role.

This Learning Short-take® combines self study with workplace activities in a unique learning system to keep you motivated and energized. So let's get started!

Step 1:
What's inside?

- Learning Short-take® Participant Guide. This section contains all of the learning content and will guide you through the learning process.
- Learning Activities. You will be prompted to complete these as you read through the Participant Guide.
- Learning Journal. This is a summary of your key learnings. Update it when prompted.
- Skill Development Action Plan. Learning is about taking action. This is your action plan where you'll plan how you will implement your learning.

Step 2:
Complete the Learning Short-take®

- Learning Short-takes® are best completed in a quiet environment that is free of distractions.
- Schedule time in your calendar to complete the Learning Short-take® and prioritize this time as an investment in your own professional development.
- Depending on the title, most participants complete the Learning Short-take® from 90 minutes to 2.5 hours.

Step 3:
Meet with your Manager/Coach

- Schedule a 30 minute meeting with your Manager or Coach.
- At this meeting share your completed Activities, Learning Journal and Skill Development Action Plan.
- Most importantly, discuss and agree on how you will implement your learning in your role.

Section 1

PARTICIPANT GUIDE

Start here →

What's in this Learning Short-take®?

"The goal as a company is to have customer service that is not just the best but legendary."

Sam Walton,
Founder of Wal-Mart

Table of Contents

How to complete your Learning Short-take®

1. Reflect on your customer service skills and abilities and how you use these to provide service excellence to your customers.

2. Complete the Initial Skills Assessment.

3. Highlight specific skill areas that you believe you could develop more. Add these to the **Learning Journal**. Add to your Learning Journal as you go.

4. When you have completed this Learning Short-take® **meet with your Manager/Coach**. In this meeting, you will jointly establish a personal **Skills Development Action Plan**.

5. Subject to your coach's final review and assessment, you will either sign off the module, or undertake further skill development as appropriate.

"It is not the strongest of the species that survives, nor the most intelligent, but the one most responsive to change."

Charles Darwin

Activity Checklist

During this Learning Short-take® you will be prompted to complete the following activities:

"It is not the employer who pays the wages. Employers only handle the money. It is the customer who pays the wages."

Henry Ford

Learning Objectives

By the end of this Learning Short-take® you should be able to:

- Define the skills and attributes of an effective customer service professional

- Explain the Customer Satisfaction Model

- Identify Customer Types and Customer Needs

- Implement strategies to retain dissatisfied customers

- Explain the 5-Step Customer Service Model

- Use superior communication skills to enhance customer interactions

"Well done is better than well said."

Benjamin Franklin

"If you do build a great experience,
customers tell each other about that.
Word of mouth is very powerful."

Jeff Bezos, CEO Amazon.com

INTRODUCING
CUSTOMER
SERVICE

Part 1

Introducing Customer Service

To maximize business success and ensure business survival, organizations must focus on their most valuable assets – their customers. The only true potential a business has lies in its customers. Those organizations who can focus their business on providing a straightforward and enjoyable experience for their customers will deliver exceptional results.

Today, the need to provide exceptional customer service is critical to business survival. It is the one competitive factor that differentiates one organization from the next. While unique products and services are an asset to any business, they no longer guarantee long term survival. Modern manufacturing, distribution and sales channels means that competition is fast and aggressive, and that while choice may be limited today, it will be widely available tomorrow. Only customer satisfaction will ensure long-term survival in this competitive marketplace.

The biggest opportunity awaiting business today is the opportunity to provide exceptional customer service, a level of service that brings the customer back again and again. Organizations must keep up with their customers changing needs and continue to satisfy them. By anticipating customer demands and expectations, organizations will continue to win their business.

Complete Activity # 1
Initial Skills Assessment

Activity 1

Initial Skills Assessment

Understanding the key elements of customer service excellence is critical to improving job and sales success. This assessment covers the core skills in providing customer service excellence in order to improve business performance.

Rate yourself on each of the techniques.

7 is competent and confident, little need for improvement

4 is average, needs improvement

1 is uncomfortable, major need for improvement

- Note specific areas of improvement related to each customer service skill that you would like to develop. Be sure to include your *reasons* for your rating in each skill, as this reasoning will be a key part of the initial goal setting session with your coach.
- Start thinking about a personal development plan and identify two things you could do to improve your skills in this area and write them in the space provided.

I...	Rating	Reasoning
provide prompt, efficient and pleasant service to every customer	1 2 3 4 5 6 7	
pay attention to all customers and do something to make them feel special	1 2 3 4 5 6 7	
recognize that customers are not always happy or pleasant, so work hard to make them feel valued	1 2 3 4 5 6 7	
always give my customers more than they expect to get	1 2 3 4 5 6 7	
consistently provide the kind of service that brings the customer back again and again	1 2 3 4 5 6 7	
embrace customers who have a grievance or complaint because I see this as an opportunity to retain their business	1 2 3 4 5 6 7	

Activity 1

Initial Skills Assessment

I...	Rating	Reasoning
build relationships with my customers by treating them as real people and not just someone who buys something from my business	1 2 3 4 5 6 7	
do not take anything for granted. I ask appropriate questions to ensure understanding of what the customer wants	1 2 3 4 5 6 7	
watch for body language signals to tell me whether my customer is happy or unhappy with the service I am providing	1 2 3 4 5 6 7	
listen carefully to my customers to ensure understanding	1 2 3 4 5 6 7	
can sum up the different types of customers that I have and identify their needs	1 2 3 4 5 6 7	
know why customers buy my organizations products and services	1 2 3 4 5 6 7	
plan for the long-term by thinking how I can serve my future customers	1 2 3 4 5 6 7	

Personal development plan ideas:

1

2

Now update your Learning Journal (page 59)

CUSTOMER SERVICE EXCELLENCE

Part 2

Customer Service Excellence

"Customer satisfaction
is first and foremost
a state of mind and
action…an every
minute of every day
obsession."

Charles M. Cawley, President of
MBNA America, Inc.

What is Customer Service Excellence?

Excellent customer service is not about doing one thing really well, but doing hundreds of small things better. It's about going the extra mile to ensure total customer satisfaction. It is adopting a customer-first approach, ensuring that you are providing the right products and services to the right people, satisfying their needs both now and in the future. It is promising what you can deliver and delivering what you promise.

The traditional approach to sales and customer service is "Here is a product or service that we can provide… now who wants to buy it?" In contrast, customer service excellence is about asking "what exactly do our customers want and need?" and "what do we need to do to be able to produce and deliver it to our customers?" This is a significant paradigm shift and a quantum leap in terms of how we look at business activity.

Not only do customers want cost-effective products or services that deliver a perceived benefit, they also want to have their needs satisfied. Customer needs extend to issues beyond the suppliers product or service proposition and include the buying process itself, how the customer service communications are handled, and the nature of the customer service relationship. This is the foundation of customer service excellence. It is integrating the customer into all aspects of the business, and developing a relationship that is deeper than the traditional 'arms-length' supplier-customer relationship.

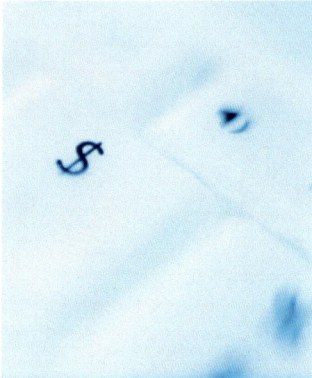

Why Provide Customer Service Excellence?

Like any organizational initiative, the ultimate goal of providing customer service excellence is to increase profit. This is achieved by providing a better service to your customers than your competitors can provide. However the provision of customer service excellence also delivers other advantages:

- It reduces costs because the right things are being done – business operation is more effective and efficient.

- There is increased customer satisfaction because customers are getting exactly what they want.

- Staff stress and turnover is reduced as the relationship with customers improves.

Why Provide Customer Service Excellence? continued

- There is improved access to market information as customers provide honest and immediate reaction to your products, services and performance.
- The business grows through positive customer referrals.
- Customers stay with the organization longer and customer attrition is lower.
- There is long term profitability and sustainability.

To ensure business longevity, relationships with customers should be ongoing, cooperative, and built for the long term. Organizations who have many transitory relationships with customers have to spend a lot of money finding new customers.

Satisfied customers who perceive a high value in your products and services make excellent advocates for your organization. These customers should be nurtured. Dissatisfied customers who perceive low value in your products and services are potential saboteurs. These customers could have little or no loyalty and may actively engage against your organization. These customers should also be nurtured to rebuild a trust relationship.

Some facts to encourage thinking

- Of all dissatisfied customers, only 4% will actually make a complaint; the other 96 % will generally go quietly away, and 91% of those will never come back.

- 68% of customers will leave because they believe that they are not valued.

- A typically dissatisfied customer tells 8 to 10 people of his or her dissatisfaction. One in five of those who are dissatisfied will tell 20 people about his or her dissatisfaction. In all, five dissatisfied customers will tell 60 people of their unhappy experience.

- It costs six times as much to attract a new customer as it does to keep an existing one.

Put customers first by always striving to deliver customer service excellence. Remember that all customers have choices. Your objective is to ensure that they continue to choose doing business with you.

Complete Activity # 2
Customer Service Excellence in Your Organization

Activity 2

Customer Service Excellence in Your Organization

What does Customer Service Excellence look like within your organization? Research your Company website, intranet site, performance competencies, or other Company literature to identify how your organization defines itself in terms of customer service. Describe how you practice these customer service attributes in your day-to-day role.

Customer Service Excellence within my organization is defined as...	I practice these customer service attributes in my day-to-day role by...

Now update your Learning Journal (page 59)

Creating Customer Satisfaction

They key to creating customer satisfaction is to recognize that customer service excellence is the one real opportunity for creating business growth and improving business performance.

Achieving customer satisfaction is all about relationships. It is how the customer feels about themselves, how they feel about you, and how they feel about the product or service they are purchasing.

Customers will buy for only two reasons, either to solve a problem, or to satisfy a need. The customer service objective is to make the customer feel good as they make their purchase decision. It is delivering the customer what they want, on their terms.

"Find out what your customers want and give it to them. If you do it again and again you will never have to worry about sales or profit."

Stew Leonard

STOP

Complete Activity # 3
Customer Service Attributes

Activity 3

Customer Service Attributes

Reflect on an experience where **you were the customer** and you received **excellent** customer service. What did the customer service person do for you that made the experience exceptional? Recall the specific behaviors that the customer service person demonstrated.

The Situation

> Describe the customer service situation.

The Behaviors

> List all of the behaviors that you observed the customer service person demonstrating in this situation.

Now go back and identify which of these behaviors are:

(1) **Skills** – the knowledge and ability to do the job and;

(2) **Attitude** – the approach to how the job is done

Use two different colored markers to distinguish *skills* from *attitudes*.

What do you notice about the results? Most of the behaviors that you observed are probably the result of a positive customer service **attitude**. The right attitude is a key ingredient to providing customer service excellence.

Now update your Learning Journal (page 59)

What Customers Want

"Start telling me…
what you will do for
me… over and over
again because you
believe I am the most
important person
in the world…
your customer."

Murray Raphel

Customers want to do business
with people:

- who will keep their word and do what
  they say they will do

- who are trustworthy and reliable

- who talk their language

- who go the extra mile to ensure they
  get what they want

- who can deliver more than what
  was promised

- who provide quality products
  and services

The Customer Satisfaction Model

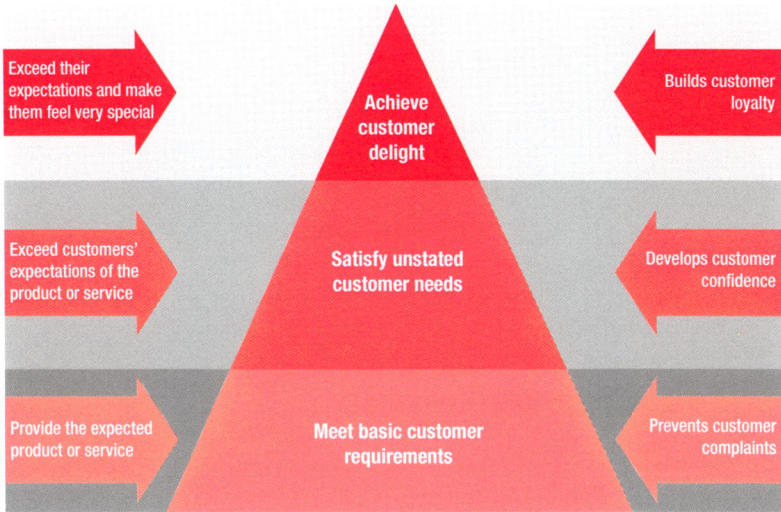

Exceed their expectations and make them feel very special → **Achieve customer delight** ← **Builds customer loyalty**

Exceed customers' expectations of the product or service → **Satisfy unstated customer needs** ← **Develops customer confidence**

Provide the expected product or service → **Meet basic customer requirements** ← **Prevents customer complaints**

Download the Customer Satisfaction Model from the TPC website at **www.tpc.net.au/tools**

Level 1: Meet Basic Customer Requirements

The first level of the Customer Satisfaction Model is to Meet Basic Customer Requirements. By meeting these requirements the customer service representative or sales person satisfies a stated customer need and prevents a customer complaint. While the goal is to move up the model, the greatest difficulty for most organizations is simply getting on to the model by meeting basic customer requirements every time.

"Most businesses aim at providing service to customers. In my view it is better to provide satisfaction. Service is decided by the giver, but satisfaction is decided by the receiver. If your customers are satisfied, you will be a winner."

Jack Collis

Level 2: Satisfy Unstated Customer Needs

The second level of the Customer Satisfaction Model is to Satisfy Unstated Customer Needs. The goal of the customer service person at this level is to help build a stronger customer relationship and increase customer confidence in them and the larger organization. The objective is to build a good reputation and increase the opportunity for repeat business.

Level 3: Delight the Customer

The third and highest level of the Customer Satisfaction Model is to Achieve Customer Delight. The goal of the customer service person at this level is to treat the customer as special by exceeding even their unstated needs. Once they reach this level, customers tend to be more forgiving because they believe that the customer service person genuinely wants to please them. If something goes wrong, the customer will assume that the problem is an exception as opposed to the norm, and will be more likely to give the individual or the organization a second chance. The objective at this level of the model is to build customer loyalty and ensure business longevity.

STOP

Complete Activity # 4
The Customer Satisfaction Model

Activity 4

The Customer Satisfaction Model

Name and describe each level of the Customer Satisfaction Model. Provide one example of how you offer satisfaction to your customers for each level of the model.

1

Level 1:

Example:

Level 2:

Example:

Level 3:

Example:

Now update your Learning Journal (page 59)

A large part of customer service success is creating a seamless experience. Customer needs are anticipated; systems are in place; employees are trained. The company runs like a well-oiled machine. But what happens when the unexpected happens? Customers have an "unusual" request or they simply don't know the rules of the system? The unexpected, I suggest, provides the opportunity to stretch the system, improve the system, or even forget the system and to Delight and Wow a customer.

1

Creative Customer Service
- How Far Will You Go to Delight a Customer?

Delight the Customer

I was speaking at a large conference in another city. I realized on the morning of the speech that I had left my contact lenses at home. I didn't want to speak on stage wearing glasses as the reflection of the lights bounced off the glass making it difficult to see. Here I was in a strange city needing new contact lenses – the impossible task!

It was Saturday morning and the hotel was about 30 minutes out of the city center. I spoke to the concierge, Mario, who explained that the stores on Saturday were only open until 12 noon and he didn't know of an optometrist close by. He asked me if I knew my prescription, I didn't (who knows that stuff!). He asked me who my optometrist was in my home town (I should have known that – but didn't!). I only remembered the optometrist's first name and the street name of the store. My presentation was at 3pm that day and it was now 9:30am.

I was expected to participate in a conference session, so left my credit card details and a desperate look of "help me" with Mario. I told him that he could put the charges onto my credit card. Off I went, hoping that Mario would magically fix it. At 11:30, I returned to Mario for an update. He had managed to get a copy of my contact lens prescription (to this day I don't know how) and was now trying to beat the clock to get the contact lenses. Again, I had to attend another conference session, so again had to leave Mario. I didn't like my chances. With 30 minutes to go before the stores closed, and 30 minutes away from the city center I was resolved to wearing my somewhat dated spectacles during my presentation.

12 noon passed – no sign of Mario. I knew the stores had now closed. At 12:30pm I checked with the front desk - another concierge informed me that Mario had finished for the day. Apparently, his shift finished at 12 noon. I hadn't had a chance to thank him for his help. I was disappointed that he hadn't told me his finish time, or come back to me to tell me that he hadn't been successful.

26

At 2:30pm I was sitting at the back of the auditorium getting ready for my presentation. I felt a tap on my shoulder and turned around to see Mario. He presented me with a small bag and said "Ms Mattiske, here are your contact lenses!" I was flabbergasted!

After my speech, I went back to the concierge desk. Mario had left for the day. To this day, I have no idea how or from where he purchased the contact lenses, or how they were paid for. The amount didn't ever appear on my credit card or on my hotel bill. When I got home, I found out there were 11 optometrists on the same street, making it even more amazing that Mario got a copy of my prescription! I wrote a letter to the hotel and I hope he was commended for his exceptional service.

Years later, Mario is probably still wowing customers in whatever role he has. Whether he stayed as concierge or is perhaps a general manager, I bet his level of customer service is still exceptional. The difference was he truly cared for my need when others might have dismissed it. He took the problem on as his own, and was determined to get a solution. He truly delighted me....the customer.

For companies with excellent systems in place, the next frontier in customer service is handling the unexpected creatively. I have observed that companies and professionals practicing creative customer service successfully have two things in common.

The first commonality is that they care. Management cares. Employees care. Everyone cares a great deal about people. They like to help people solve problems. The concierge at the hotel cared about my contact lens predicament and personally decided to go above and beyond. How much does your company care? How much do you care?

The second commonality is that employees have authority. Even when people care, if their hands are tied they can't help. In addition, employees who aren't especially "caring" might be motivated to be creative for customers simply because it feels good to exercize their authority. Do you have enough authority to be creative?

With all of the advances in technology, doing a good job isn't good enough to separate from the pack.

How far will you go to delight a customer?

> "The single most important thing to remember about any enterprise is that there are no results inside its walls. The result of a business is a satisfied customer."
>
> Peter Drucker

How do you move up the Customer Satisfaction Model?

Moving up the pyramid of customer satisfaction requires an ongoing commitment to meeting and exceeding customer needs and expectations. Given that customer needs are continually changing it is vital that you understand your customers thoroughly, listen to them regularly, watch for developments or events that affect them and their business, and plan for future requirements.

It is also important to recognize that the expectations of different customers for the same product or service will vary according to social and demographic factors, economic situation, educational standards, competitor products, and experience. Given these variables, you need to find out why your customers do business with you. Tune into the relevant relationship drivers and find out what service features keep your customers loyal to you.

Every organization has areas where it is already delighting customers and other areas where it is failing to meet even the most basic customer requirements.

While the goal is to move up each level, the challenge for most organizations is getting on to the model in the first place and meeting basic customer requirements 100% of the time.

Even where an organization achieves customer delight and becomes a leader in its field, it still needs to continually find better ways of responding to changing requirements.

1

"The purpose of business is to create customers. Customers create profits. Business survives only on its customers."

Peter Drucker

1

"Loyal customers, they don't just come back, they don't simply recommend you, they insist that their friends do business with you."

Chip Bell, Founder Chip Bell Group

30

UNDERSTANDING CUSTOMER TYPES

Part 3

Customer Types
and Customer Needs

Every business has two types of customer:

The External Customer	The Internal Customer
The people who buy the products or services of the business and on whom the business depends for survival. External Customers are where the business must place its focus because they are the profit drivers. To do this effectively the business relies on the expertize and commitment of the customer within. Examples of External Customers may be the customer who walks into your retail store, the customer who orders product online, the customer who phones for a quote or the customer who has a service issue.	The people within the organization who provide the energy and know-how that keep the organization functioning and who make it possible to serve the external customer. These are the people who manage the business, develop its products and services, sell or deliver products and services, and provide a host of other skills essential to the operation of the business. Examples of Internal Customers include your manager, the people who manage the business, develop its products and services, sell or deliver products and services and provide a host of other skills essential to the operation of the business.

These customer types can be further broken down into:

Direct Customers	Indirect Customers
Those with whom you have direct contact or interaction. For example: a customer who is in your store, a customer who calls you, a customer to whom you send product.	People with whom you do not have direct contact but who still contribute to the financial success of the business (external) or who make it possible to provide a product or service (internal). For example: a customer who buys the products for someone else to use, the customer's manager who may influence the sale, the person in accounts payable who pays the invoice that you've given to your customer.

Focusing on Your Best Customers

Whether your customers are internal to your organization, outside the organization, or representatives of other organizations, some will be better prospects than others. Your best customers are not necessarily the ones who bring you the greatest profits now, but those who will want more of your products or services in the future.

It is more cost-effective to retain existing customers than to attract new ones so focus on those who are likely to provide the best returns in the future. Therefore it makes sense to retain your best customers by anticipating new economic conditions and helping current customers adapt to them.

Pareto's Law (The Pareto Principle)

Pareto's Law is commonly known as the 80:20 rule. Typically in any organization:

- 20% of customers account for 80% of your turnover
- 20% of customers account for 80% of your profits
- 20% of customers account for 80% of your service and supply problems

It is important to know which customers fit into which category and then to manage them accordingly.

Customer Needs

1 While the reasons people give for buying a product or service are varied, all of them fall into a category of either satisfying a need or solving a problem. Customers also buy for emotional reasons. In addition to buying products for what they are; they also buy them for how they make them feel.

While customer needs vary from person to person, they can generally be defined as either 'surface' or 'human needs'. **Surface** needs are about owning the product or service that your business sells, purely for the function that the product or service provides. For example, the need to purchase car insurance in the event of an accident.

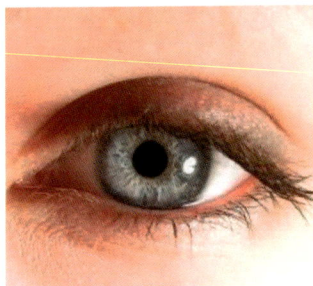

Human needs are the emotional needs that customers develop as a result of purchasing a particular product or service. These include the need for timely service, to feel important and valued as a customer, to be understood, to feel comfortable, to be appreciated, to receive assistance, etc.

Complete Activity # 5
Customer Types and Customer Needs

Complete Activity # 6 & 7
Customer Service Needs – Case Studies

Activity 5

Customer Types and Customer Needs

Step 1: Write the definition of Direct and Indirect, External and Internal customers in the space provided.

Step 2: List your specific customers or customer groups and identify them as either Direct External, Indirect External, Direct Internal or Indirect Internal.

		Direct	**Indirect**
		Write definition here	Write definition here
External	Write definition here		
Internal	Write definition here		

Activity 5

Customer Types and Customer Needs

1

For each Customer Type, identify their Needs and how you can help meet these needs.

Customer Type	Needs	How can I help?
Direct External		
Indirect External		
Direct Internal		
Indirect Internal		

Now update your Learning Journal (page 59)

Activity 6

Customer Service Needs: Case Study # 1 - John

John is on the Information Desk of a large city bank. While serving a busy lunchtime customer line he notices an elderly woman entering the bank. She stands just inside the door, looks around for a while and then goes over to the list of services board display and studies it closely.

After checking her passbook details, she hesitantly heads towards the Information Desk, clutching her passbook and some money. She waits in line for about five minutes and then finally approaches John and says:

"I'm sorry to bother you, young man, but I think I may need some help. I've got a little bit of money here that I would like to put aside for a rainy day, but my daughter thinks I can do better than just put it in my usual Savings Account. Is that right?"

What are this customer's main needs? (Check ☑ the appropriate boxes)

The need for timely service. ☐

The need to feel welcome. ☐

The need to feel important. ☐

The need to be understood. ☐

The need to be comfortable. ☐

The need for efficient and orderly service. ☐

The need to receive assistance. ☐

The need for appreciation. ☐

Which of the following responses would be appropriate for John to do in this instance?

1. Glance at the name in the passbook and use it as he speaks to her. ☐
2. Ask questions about how much she wishes to invest and for how long. ☐
3. Tell her he would prefer to be called by his name rather than as "young man". ☐
4. Give her a leaflet on the different types of accounts available. ☐
5. Smile and reassure her that he will be happy to help. ☐
6. Speak slowly and clearly. ☐
7. Pull out a form for a Term Investment Account and begin to fill it in. ☐
8. Ask her to come back at a quieter time. ☐
9. Explain that there are several different types of accounts and that he considers it important that she finds the right one for her needs. ☐
10. Ask another assistant to take her to a quiet cubicle to discuss the matter. ☐

Activity 6

Suggested Answers: Case Study # 1 - John

1

The elderly bank customer's main needs are:

The need to feel welcome.	☑
The need to be understood.	☑
The need to be comfortable.	☑
The need to receive assistance.	☑

The appropriate responses for John would be:

1. Glance at the name in the passbook and use it as he speaks to her. ☑
2. Ask questions about how much she wishes to invest and for how long. ☑
3. Tell her he would prefer to be called by his name rather than as "young man". ☐
4. Give her a leaflet on the different types of accounts available. ☐
5. Smile and reassure her that he will be happy to help. ☑
6. Speak slowly and clearly. ☑
7. Pull out a form for a Term Investment Account and begin to fill it in. ☐
8. Ask her to come back at a quieter time. ☐
9. Explain that there are several different types of accounts and that he considers it important that she finds the right one for her needs. ☑
10. Ask another assistant to take her to a quiet cubicle to discuss the matter. ☐

Now update your Learning Journal (page 59)

38

Activity 7

Customer Service Needs: Case Study # 2 - Elizabeth

Elizabeth is the receptionist for a large company. She is expected to complete other office duties as well as attend to all visitors to the building. This morning she is busy inputting data into the computer. The work has to be completed within the next half hour.

Suddenly a man rushes through the entrance doors and strides towards her desk. He is wearing a dark, conservative suit with designer shirt and cufflinks. His neat leather briefcase is boldly embossed in gold with his initials. He is glancing at his watch and says.

"Robert Filmeld. STR Consultants. I have an appointment with Ken Dawson in two minutes."

What are Robert Filmeld's main needs?   (Check ☑ the appropriate boxes)

The need for timely service.	☐
The need to feel welcome.	☐
The need to feel important.	☐
The need to be understood.	☐
The need to be comfortable.	☐
The need for efficient and orderly service.	☐
The need to receive assistance.	☐
The need for appreciation.	☐

Which of the following responses would be appropriate for Elizabeth to do in this instance?

1. Ask him to take a seat while she checks with Ken's receptionist that he is expected. ☐
2. Ask him to fill in the Visitors' Book while she phones to check Ken is available. ☐
3. Ask if Robert would mind waiting a minute as she is in the middle of an entry. ☐
4. Smile and ask him how his day is going. ☐
5. Explain that she thinks Ken has just left the building, but that she will check anyway. ☐
6. Hold confident eye contact with Robert as she directs him to Ken's office. ☐
7. Ask Robert the purpose of his visit. ☐
8. Read Robert's name as he fills in the book and use it as she directs him to Ken's office. ☐
9. Discuss the weather and ask if he had any trouble finding the building. ☐
10. Show she is efficient by carrying on with her computer work while she telephones Ken's secretary and while Robert fills in the Visitors' Book. ☐

1

The customer's main needs are:

The need for timely service.	☑
The need to feel important.	☑
The need for efficient and orderly service.	☑

The appropriate responses for Elizabeth would be:

1. Ask him to take a seat while she checks with Ken's receptionist that he is expected. ☐
2. Ask him to fill in the Visitors' Book while she phones to check Ken is available. ☑
3. Ask if Robert would mind waiting a minute as she is in the middle of an entry. ☐
4. Smile and ask him how his day is going. ☐
5. Explain that she thinks Ken has just left the building, but that she will check anyway. ☐
6. Hold confident eye contact with Robert as she directs him to Ken's office. ☑
7. Ask Robert the purpose of his visit. ☐
8. Read Robert's name as he fills in the book and use it as she directs him to Ken's office. ☑
9. Discuss the weather and ask if he had any trouble finding the building. ☐
10. Show she is efficient by carrying on with her computer work while she telephones Ken's secretary and while Robert fills in the Visitors' Book. ☐

Now update your Learning Journal (page 59)

5-STEP CUSTOMER SERVICE MODEL

Part 4

The 5-Step
Customer Service Model

1

Step 1:
Create the Right Environment

Step 2:
Start the Conversation:
Uncover needs

Step 3:
Propose the Solution

Step 4:
Delight the Customer

Step 5:
Leave a Lasting Good Impression

Download the 5-Step Customer Service Model from
the TPC website at **www.tpc.net.au/tools**

Complete Activity # 8
The 5-Step Customer Service Model

Activity 8

The 5-Step Customer Service Model

Describe how you go about achieving each of the 5-Steps to provide
Customer Service Excellence in your current role. Hints have been provided to help spark ideas.

1

Step 1: Create the Right Environment

I achieve this by….

HINT…

- Be polite
- Smile
- Shake hands
- Make eye contact

Step 2: Start the Conversation: Uncover needs

I achieve this by….

HINT…

- Engage the customer
- Listen and ask questions
- Don't assume anything
- Treat each customer as an individual

Activity 8

The 5-Step Customer Service Model

1

Step 3: Propose the Solution

> I achieve this by….

HINT…

- Work through the options with your customer
- Agree a solution
- Repeat for complete understanding

Step 4: Delight the Customer

> I achieve this by….

HINT…

- Sell
- Upsell
- Close
- Provide the agreed level of service

Step 5: Leave a Lasting Good Impression

> I achieve this by….

HINT…

- Last comment/phrase to customer
- Follow-up call/email/communication
- On-going communication

Now update your Learning Journal (page 59)

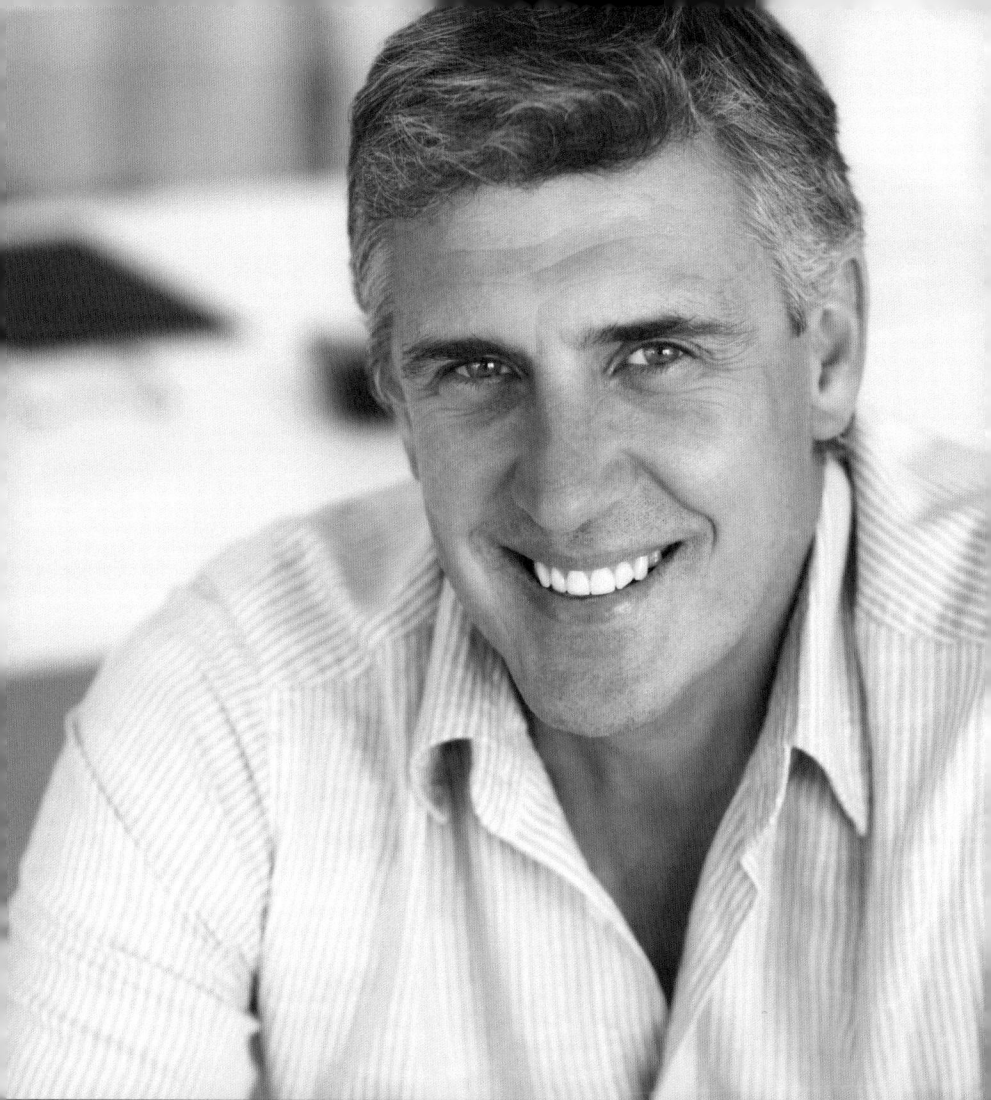

HANDLING DIFFICULT CUSTOMER ENCOUNTERS

Part 5

Dealing with Customer Complaints & Calming Upset Customers

A customer complaint is an excellent opportunity to learn, improve your customer service, and find out what customers really want.

Canvassing dissatisfied customers could potentially be one of the most profitable activities a business undertakes. Welcome complaints as a chance to impress your customers and encourage their loyalty, while looking for opportunities to prevent the problem from occurring again.

"You should love complaints more than compliments. A complaint is someone letting you know that you haven't satisfied them yet. They have gold written all over them."

Donald L. Beaver, Jr

46

Customers who are motivated to complain are giving you a chance to put things right. This means that if you handle the complaint effectively, you are more likely to retain the customer and even improve the customer relationship.

When customers complain, it is because they believe that they have been treated unfairly. When a complaint arises, there are two factors to be considered – the first is the customer, and the second is the complaint itself. Understanding why customers are angry and making them feel better is not the same thing.

Simply solving the problem of a faulty product or a failure of the business to provide an expected service, does not always overcome negative customer emotions. It is possible to fix the problem and still lose the customer unless particular attention is paid to the customer's feelings.

"Your most unhappy customers are your greatest source of learning."

Bill Gates

How the customer is treated at the time of the complaint is the critical factor in resolving the problem. If the complaint becomes a contest to find a winner, then the outcome has already been decided.

The business will always lose when being 'right' is considered more important than preserving the customer relationship. It is imperative that customer service representatives and sales professionals always work with the aim of preserving the relationship over winning an argument with a customer.

"Nothing is ever gained by winning an argument and losing a customer."

C. F. Norton

Complete Activity # 9
Dealing with Customer Complaints

Activity 9

Dealing with Customer Complaints

Reflect on a situation where **you are serving a customer** and a customer has made a complaint. Answer the following:

Describe the situation.

What was the outcome of the situation?

What would you do differently if faced with a similar situation?

What did you learn from this experience?

Now update your Learning Journal (page 59)

7 Steps for Calming Upset Customers

1. **Treat Complainants as Valued Customers**. Any time you spend on repairing the customer's feelings will be productive. Address customers by name.

2. **Listen**. Listen actively to what your customer is saying. Let the customer talk. Ask questions to ensure understanding. Be patient and hear the customer out. Don't be defensive or take criticism personally.

3. **Restate the Concern**. Be sure to get all relevant information and repeat it to the customer to gain agreement.

4. **Offer One Apology**. The customer will want to hear you take responsibility for the situation even if it was not your fault. "I'm terribly sorry you are upset" does not admit blame, however does establish rapport with the customer. Don't make excuses or blame others in your organization.

5. **Offer a Solution**. When you are able, offer a solution that meets the expectations of the customer. Ensure that any solution is specific so that the customer is left in no doubt as to how the issue will be resolved. If a solution is becoming difficult ask the customer what they think a fair outcome would be. In the majority of cases , the customer will require you to do less than you were willing to do, so accepting the solution should be less difficult.

6. **Implement**. Carry out an action plan to rectify a situation to agreed standards and schedules. Summarize what you plan to do to ensure successful implementation, and any actions for the customer. Include and gain agreement to any actions that need to be carried out by staff in other departments.

7. **Follow Up**. Ensure that the complaint has been resolved to the customer's full satisfaction. Check with the customer if there is anything further that you can do for them. Examine the underlying cause of the complaint to ensure that it doesn't occur again.

Download the 7-Step Handling Difficult Situations Model from the TPC website at www.tpc.net.au/tools

COMMUNICATING WITH CUSTOMERS

Part 5

Customer Service Communication Skills

Customers communicate with a business in a variety of ways, but the majority of two-way communications are carried out either by phone, written, or face-to-face.

Tips for Telephone Communication

- **Answer all calls promptly and identify yourself and your organization.**

- **Be friendly, courteous and professional.** Check your attitude regularly to ensure politeness.

- **Don't keep customers on hold.** If you have to place a customer on hold for any reason, go back at regular intervals and advise the caller what is happening. Always give the caller the option of leaving a message or having someone else attend the call.

- **Make sure that you understand what the caller wants.** If you are unable to help, then make sure you transfer the caller to someone who can. If necessary, call the person you think can help and ensure that they can in fact do so. Take responsibility for ensuring that the caller achieves customer satisfaction and do not assume that you have done your part simply by transferring the call.

- **Take responsibility for solving caller complaints personally, or find someone who can.**

Tips for Written Communication

■ **Promptly respond to written communication from customers.** Nothing upsets customers more than being ignored. When a customer contacts a business in writing they expect a prompt reply. If it is not possible to respond quickly, call the customer and explain the reason for the delay, and confirm when they can expect to hear from you again.

■ **Ensure that the customers name is spelled correctly and personal details are accurate.** Nothing devalues a customer more than a letter arriving with the customers name spelled incorrectly, or with an incorrect address. Ensure that your records are accurate and up to date.

■ **Ensure that any information contained in a letter is easy to understand ie. simple language, simple layout, logical etc.** Also ensure that it communicates a message to the customer that they are valued.

■ **Be clear about who has written the letter – sign the letter and provide a typewritten name below.** The customer must know who signed the letter and how they can communicate with the writer.

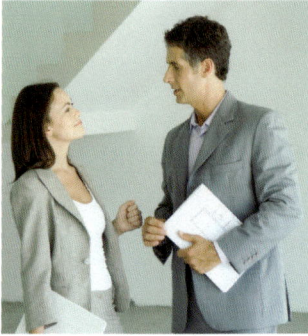

"Spend a lot of time talking to customers face to face. You'd be amazed how many companies don't listen to their customers."

Ross Perot

Tips for Face-to-Face Communication

- **Greet the customer immediately and make eye contact.** First impressions are critical.

- **Never ignore a customer.** Every customer service person should make it an absolute rule that as soon as they see a customer needing attention, they stop doing other work or break off their conversation with other employees, to attend immediately to the customer.

- **Be yourself with the customer.** Act naturally and be consistent. Be friendly, energetic and enthusiastic. Make each moment of customer contact a positive one for you and for the business.

- **Find out and understand what the customer wants.** Do so in a way that will ensure your customers think they are receiving all of your attention. Ask questions that show you want to be involved. Feed back to customers what you believe they have said, and then ask for confirmation that you have understood them correctly.

Tips for All Customer Communication

- **Use the customer's name.** When the customer's name is used in a courteous and friendly manner it has great power to create the right atmosphere in which to start, conduct and complete a business transaction.

- **Act on the customer's behalf – remember it is customer who is paying your salary.** Make their problems your problems, and act as if what is happening to them is happening to you, then arrange an appropriate solution.

- **Never hide behind the rule book.** Nothing upsets customers more than having someone quote the rule book at them. Customers are not interested in the rules of your business or the reason that you have them – they are interested only in solving their own problems. Policies and procedures should be made to encourage customers, not deter them from doing business with you.

- **Know your products and services well.** It is not sufficient just to know where these products and services are; it is necessary to know how they work and how they compare with competitor products. Customers expect to get answers and information on the products and services that your business provides and become increasingly frustrated when the person with whom they are dealing is unable to adequately assist them.

- **Leave your customer with a good impression of you and your business.** How you complete your work with your customer is just as important as how you began. What you do just prior to completing business with them has a huge bearing on whether they will come back again. Invite your customers back again and ensure that they know how and where to find you. Have customers leave with the feeling that they are valued, and that the time they spent with you has been well spent.

Complete Activity # 10
Customer Service Communication Skills

Activity 10

Customer Service Communication Skills

1 From the previous pages, select two communication skills tips from each category and explain how you will go about implementing these tips in your day-to-day role.

Tips for Telephone Communication

Tip 1:
I will implement this tip by…

Tip 2:
I will implement this tip by…

Tips for Written Communication

Tip 1:
I will implement this tip by…

Tip 2:
I will implement this tip by…

Activity 10

Customer Service Communication Skills

1

Tips for Face-to-Face Communication

Tip 1:

I will implement this tip by…

Tip 2:

I will implement this tip by…

Tips for All Customer Communication

Tip 1:

I will implement this tip by…

Tip 2:

I will implement this tip by…

Now update your Learning Journal (page 59)

Remember Me

"I'm the person who goes into a restaurant, sits down patiently and waits while the waitress does everything but take my order.

I'm the fellow who goes into a store and stands quietly while the counter until staff finish their little chit-chat.

I'm the person who drives into a service station and never blows the horn, but waits patiently while the attendant finishes reading his book.

Yes, you might say I'm a good guy.
But do you know who else I am?

I'm the customer who never comes back, and it amuses me to see you spending thousands of dollars every year to get me back when I was there in the first place ....

and all you had to do was show me a little courtesy."

Section 2

LEARNING JOURNAL

The Learning Journal is used throughout the Learning Short-take® process to record your key learnings, hot tips and things to remember.

Update your Learning Journal at anytime throughout the Learning Short-take® process. Ensure you complete your Learning Journal after you finish each activity. Then turn back to the Participant Guide to continue your learning.

Learning Journal

As you work through this Learning Short-take®, make detailed notes on this page of the lessons you have learned and any useful skill areas. For each lesson or refresher point think about how you could further develop this skill. Your coach will want to discuss these with you in your Skill Development Action Planning meeting.

"…that is what learning is.
You suddenly understand something you've understood all your life, but in a new way."

Doris Lessing

"Act as though it were impossible to fail. "

Winston Churchill

"The wise do at once what the fool does later."
Baltasar Gracian (1601-58), Spanish Jesuit priest and author.

Learning or Idea	Action to be taken	Result Expected

Learning Journal - continued

Learning or Idea	Action to be taken	Result Expected

"Anyone who stops learning is old, whether at twenty or eighty."
Henry Ford

Learning or Idea	Action to be taken	Result Expected

2

"Customer service is just a day in, day
out ongoing, never ending, unremitting,
persevering, compassionate,
type of activity."

Leon Gorman, CEO L.L.Bean

Section 3

SKILL DEVELOPMENT ACTION PLAN

Your Skill Development Action Plan is the last Step in the Learning Short-take® process. After you have completed the Participant Guide and all Activities update your Learning Journal then complete this section.

Skill Development Action Plan

This is the most important part of the program - your individual Skill Development Action Plan.

You need to complete this plan before meeting with your manager or prior to on-going coaching. You will discuss it in detail with your manager or coach as he or she will ensure that you have everything you need to complete the tasks and activities.

Once you have completed your **Skill Development Action Plan** schedule a meeting time with your manager or coach to review your plan. Take your participant guide and all other documentation received during the training course to this meeting.

Remember - you have committed to your **Skill Development Action Plan**, and need to make time to complete your tasks!

"The mind, once stretched by a new idea, never regains its original dimensions."

Oliver Wendell Holmes

"Whatever you can do or dream you can - begin it. Boldness has genius, power and magic."

Johann Wolfgang von Goethe

"Imagination is the eye of the soul."
Joseph Joubert (1754-1824)

Task or activity (Be specific)	Measure (this will help you to know you have achieved it)	Date (Be specific)
Reflect on your Learning Journal. Transfer action items that you can apply to your job. Ensure that you include some 'stretch goals' and also a blend of short, medium and long term goals.	Apart from you, who else is needed to assist you in achieving your goal.	Be specific. A general date such as 'Quarter 1', 'August', or 'by end of year' is vague and more likely to result in not achieving your target. Be specific – e.g. 22nd November.

3

Ideas for discussion with my manager

Ideas

Congratulations!

You've now completed this Learning Short-take®.

Meet with your Manager/Coach to discuss your
Skill Development Action Plan.

"For us, our most important stakeholder is not our stockholders, it is our customers. We're in business to serve the needs and desires of our core customer base."

John Mackey

extra

QUICK
REFERENCE

This Quick Reference provides you with a summary of key concepts, models and reference material from Learning Short-takes®. We have also included some quotations to ponder.

Use this section as a quick reference to keep your learning active.

4

> ❝ **The purpose of business is to create customers. Customers create profits. Business survives only on its customers.** ❞

Peter Drucker

Customer Service Excellence

Excellent customer service is not about doing one thing really well, but doing hundreds of small things better. It's about going the extra mile to ensure total customer satisfaction.

Four Customer Types

	DIRECT	**INDIRECT**
EXTERNAL	External customers with whom YOU have contact – those who get your product or service.	External customers with whom only SOME people interact with yet they contribute to the success of the business.
INTERNAL	People within the company with whom YOU interact – those who get your product or service.	People within the company that make it possible for us to provide service e.g. Accounts, HR.

Dissatisfied Customers

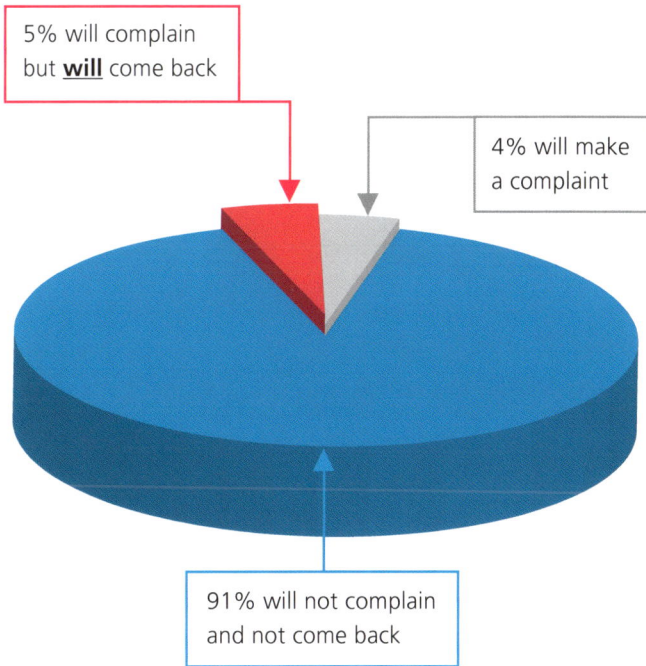

4

5% will complain but **will** come back

4% will make a complaint

91% will not complain and not come back

4

> **" You should love complaints more than compliments.**
> **A complaint is someone letting you know that you haven't satisfied them yet.**
> **They have gold written all over them. "**
>
> Donald L Beaver, Jr

Quick Reference

The Customer Satisfaction Model

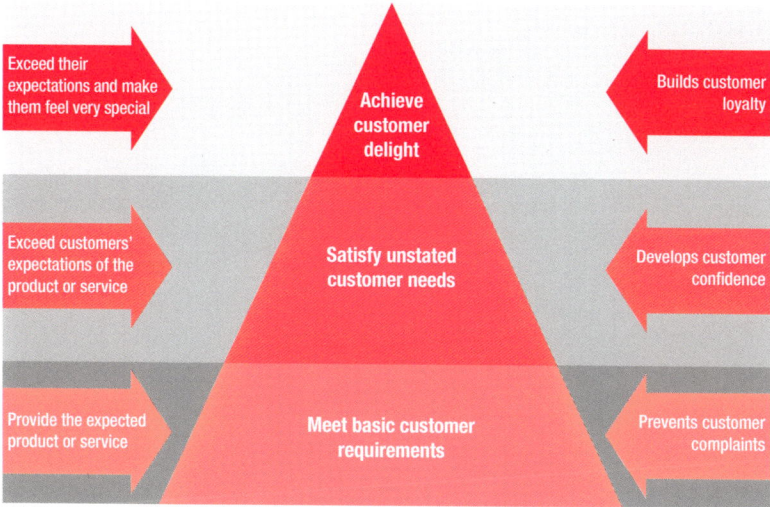

- Exceed their expectations and make them feel very special
- Achieve customer delight
- Builds customer loyalty
- Exceed customers' expectations of the product or service
- Satisfy unstated customer needs
- Develops customer confidence
- Provide the expected product or service
- Meet basic customer requirements
- Prevents customer complaints

4

4

> ❝ **Find out what your customers want and give it to them. If you do it again and again you will never have to worry about sales or profit.** ❞
>
> Stew Leonard

7 Steps for Calming Upset Customers

1. Treat Complainants as Valued Customers

2. Listen

3. Restate the Concern

4. Offer One Apology

5. Offer a Solution

6. Implement

7. Follow-Up

4

" **Biggest question: Isn't it really 'customer helping' rather than customer service? And wouldn't you deliver better service if you thought of it that way?** "

Jeffrey Gitomer

Tips for Telephone Communication

- Answer all calls promptly
- Be friendly, courteous and professional
- Don't keep customers on hold
- Make sure that you understand what the caller wants
- Take responsibility for solving caller complaints personally, or find someone who can

4

4

> **" Although your customers won't love you if you give bad service, your competitors will. "**
>
> Kate Zabriskie

Tips for Written Communication

- Promptly respond to written communication from customers

- Ensure that the customers name is spelled correctly and personal details are accurate

- Ensure that any information contained in a letter is easy to understand

- Be clear about who has written the letter - sign the letter and provide a typewritten name below

4

" Customers don't expect you to be perfect. They do expect you to fix things when they go wrong. "

Donald Porter

Tips for Face-to-Face Communication

- Greet the customer immediately and make eye contact

- Never ignore a customer

- Be yourself with the customer

- Find out and understand what the customer wants

4

4

" Maybe 'Customer Service' should be more than one department. "

SAP ad

Tips for All Communication

- Use the customer's name
- Act on the customers behalf
- Never hide behind the rule book or the policy
- Know your products and services well
- Leave your customer with a good impression of you and your business

4

4

" There are no traffic jams along the extra mile. "

Roger Staubach

5-Step Customer Service Model

Step 1:
Create the Right Environment

4

Step 2:
Start the Conversation:
Uncover needs

Step 3:
Propose the Solution

Step 4:
Delight the Customer

Step 5:
Leave a Lasting Good Impression

"A lot of companies have chosen to downsize, and maybe that was the right thing for them. We chose a different path. Our belief was that if we kept putting great products in front of customers, they would continue to open their wallets."

Steve Jobs

NEXT STEPS

Congratulations! You have now completed this Learning Short-take®
title. The entire list of Learning Short-takes® can be found on the
TPC website.

In this section we have suggested Learning Short-take® titles for
you that will build your learning. You may order these Learning
Short-takes® online at www.tpc.net.au or from your bookstores.

Understanding Relationship Selling
How to Build Customer's Rapport, Respect & Trust

Learning Short-take® Outline

Understanding Relationship Selling combines self-study with realistic workplace activities to develop skills in understanding the value of building relationships with your customers to facilitate repeat business and achieve referrals. It compares traditional selling techniques with more modern sales processes based on the development of trust, rapport and empathy. This Learning Short-take® will guide you in evaluating your own approach to selling, and help you develop new and innovative strategies to foster key relationships, understand customer needs, and provide appropriate sales solutions.

Relationship selling is based on the premise that the best source of new business is through existing customers and referrals from existing customers. This approach requires a long-term commitment to providing ongoing customer satisfaction, rather than just a short-term focus on making sales. While relationship selling may take longer to cultivate, the organization will be rewarded with high levels of repeat business, new business and referrals from satisfied customers.

Understanding Relationship Selling includes the **'Relationship Selling' Job Aid**, provided as a free downloadable tool.

Learning Objectives

- Define relationship selling.
- Explain the difference between traditional selling and relationship selling.
- State key differences between product-based selling and needs-based selling.
- Explain the importance of trust in relationship selling.
- Explain the principles of relationship selling.
- Describe how to maintain a relationship even when the answer is 'no'.
- Identify the steps in the relationship selling process.
- Create a Skill Development Action.

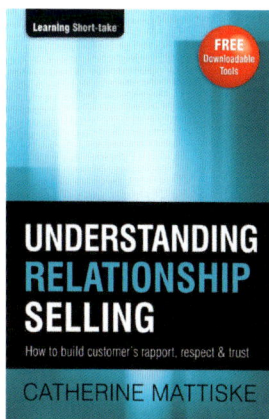

Course Content

- Part 1: Traditional versus modern approaches to selling
- Part 2: Evolution of the selling function
- Part 3: Inside the sales call
- Part 4: Principles of relationship selling
- Part 5: Relationship builders and relationship breakers
- Part 6: Top ten tips for relationship selling

Effective Time Management
Clear the Clutter and Focus on What's Important

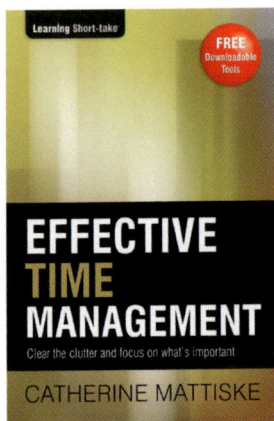

Learning Short-take® Outline

Effective Time Management combines self-study with realistic workplace activities to provide the key skills and techniques that allow you to manage your time more effectively. You will learn to do the things you 'have to do' more efficiently, and generate more time for the things you 'want to do'. You will learn tips, tricks and techniques to ensure a positive return on your investment in time, increasing success in both your work and personal life.

Time is our most unique and valuable resource. We all have 24 hours in a day, 168 hours in a week, and we spend it at the same rate. Time management is about more than time - it is really about managing our lives. **Effective Time Management** will assist you to balance priorities, achieve more, be more efficient and learn to maximize minutes!

Effective Time Management includes the **Daily To Do List** and the **Weekly Planner**, provided to you as free downloadable tools.

Course Content

- Part 1: Getting Started
- Part 2: Time Matrix
- Part 3: Daily and Weekly Actions
- Part 4: Tips and Traps
- Part 5: A Final Thought

Learning Objectives

- Identify your own habits and time management behavior.
- Set short, medium and long term goals.
- Weed out tasks that are unimportant or a waste of time.
- Prioritize your work and create daily and weekly planners.
- Make instant changes to your workspace.
- Handle interruptions and avoid sidetracks.

Understanding Customer Motivation
Get Inside the Customer's Mind

Learning Short-take® Outline

Understanding Customer Motivation combines self-study with real workplace activities to help you understand the key elements that motivate customers. You will learn specific techniques to encourage your customers to start or continue to do business with you and to provide them with the products and services that they need. **Understanding Customer Motivation** investigates the importance of creating value for customers, why customers buy, the impact and influences of buying objectives, the four customer types, adapting the selling process, and a process for identifying value opportunities in your business.

Customers are interested in products and services that fulfill their needs and wants. If a customer doesn't have a perceived need or want, then it is unlikely that they will buy. As an experienced salesperson, you will appreciate the importance of need creation in motivating customers to want to own or use the products and services that you sell. By examining the psychology and critical motivators of buying, **Understanding Customer Motivation** will assist you in garnering new and recurring customers and preserving positive customer relationships.

Understanding Customer Motivation includes the **Value Identification Tool** and the **True Motivators Reminder Card**, provided as free downloadable tools.

Learning Objectives

- Explain the psychology of buying and the elements of customer motivation.
- Explain the importance of creating value for customers and the impact on customer motivation.
- Identify value opportunities in your business.
- Explain why customers buy and the impact of buying objectives and buying influences.
- Develop strategies for aligning customer behavior types with need creation opportunities.
- Create a Skill Development Action Plan.

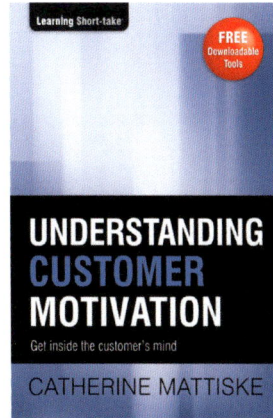

Course Content

- Part 1: Getting Started
- Part 2: Psychology of Buying
- Part 3: Why Customers Buy
- Part 4: Theories of Motivation
- Part 5: 7 Service Principles
- Part 6: Customer Types

TPC - The Performance Company is known world wide as 'the place to go' for Corporate Training Courses, e-Learning, Train the Trainer and Instructional Design Programs.

Corporate Training Division

> Global Learning Platform - Coordinate your training worldwide
> Instructional Design - Customized instructor-led and e-Learning courses for your organization
> Trainer Development - Maximize your training effectiveness
> Coaching - Get the best from your participants
> Strategic Consulting - Helping clients meet their goals

Learning Short-takes® Division

> Professional Development
> Sales and Customer Service
> Leadership and Management
> Trainer Development
> Able to be customized for individual clients

www.tpc.net.au

New York   •   California   •   Sydney